THE VOLCANO'S

HIGH HELD

SNOW NOTE

BOOKS BY TIM LILBURN

Names of God (1986)
Tourist to Ecstasy (1989)
From the Great Above She Opened Her Ear to the Great Below (with Susan Shantz) (1991)
Moosewood Sandhills (1994)
To the River (1999)
Living In The World As If It Were Home (1999)
Kill-site (2003)
Desire Never Leaves: The Poetry of Tim Lilburn (with Alison Calder) (2006)
Orphic Politics (2008)
Going Home: Essays (2008)
Assiniboia (2012)
The Names (2016)
The Larger Conversation: Contemplation and Place (2017)
The House of Charlemagne (2018)
Harmonia Mundi (2022)
Numinous Seditions: Interiority and Climate Change (2023)

The Volcano's High Held Snow Note

POEMS

TIM LILBURN

McClelland & Stewart

The authorized representative in the EU for product safety and compliance is Penguin Random House Ireland, Morrison Chambers, 32 Nassau Street, Dublin D02 YH68, Ireland, https://eu-contact.penguin.ie

LIBRARY AND ARCHIVES CANADA CATALOGUING IN PUBLICATION
Title: The volcano's high held snow note : poems / Tim Lilburn.
Names: Lilburn, Tim, 1950- author.
Identifiers: Canadiana (print) 20260151440 | Canadiana (ebook) 20260152463 | ISBN 9780771026584 (softcover) | ISBN 9780771026676 (EPUB)
Subjects: LCGFT: Poetry.
Classification: LCC PS8573.I427 V65 2026 | DDC C811/.54—dc23

Cover design by Andrew Roberts
Cover art: (mountain) Doa Bunda, (snow) JIRMoronta / Adobe Stock
Typeset in Fournier by Daniella Zanchetta and Six Red Marbles
Printed in the United States of America

McClelland & Stewart
A division of Penguin Random House Canada
320 Front Street West, Suite 1400
Toronto, Ontario, M5V 3B6, Canada
penguinrandomhouse.ca

1st Printing

Penguin Random House
McCLELLAND & STEWART

Contents

THE VOLCANO'S

HIGH HELD

SNOW NOTE

NOW, HE THINKS

The child puts up his hand
to stand as an ear vortexing
over rising basalt.
What else?
Can anything more winningly blue
come his way? He's in.
A notetaker of afternoons and
Mars rising.
What else? He hunches
near the biggest oak
and takes his time.

COLD

Matted snow with hard crust
unfolds, linen cloth, on the west face,
the male hummingbird broken
from sleep, its seal,
stilled at the just thawed feeder.

Final dark, snow
breathes down between monstrous firs,
the cat door in the shed blocked by snow
and the death seven years ago of the ingenious cat.

I speak the magical language to the male
to warm him. Puffed, enflamed
on the dead cedar branch, his eye on me and
the door from where comes
anagogic liquid.

LITTLE GREETING

Angel of the cliff rock, *mirabundus*,
with another language;
mind of rotting pink,
ironwood shag bloom,
speech, rilling acetylene feather;
sent mind
of the oak, the red vein
in blue spruce in cool, dry July.
The oak, its eyes.

THEN

Here is where you were coming back then
pocked, black-purple Big Quill Lake, wind-accordioned.
To enlist here in the early fall
was the plan.
Lodged, javelin forehead
driven, in a slope dug-out,
clothed and bedded with echoing damp
and roots inches up from halitotic water,
swans swaying in, weight-growing with speed,
to land,
pounding, rubbled roof.
Eye houses everywhere.
Nights in the mouths of stars.

You'd live in the processional slough-
edge ground below a door opening upward
to Orion's belt,
elk and deer drinking at the crusty shore,
no sickness in their bodies. That
mist coming off them.

HOW IT WOULD BE

Wolves and silence.
Hungry star. A second or third
winter on the tip of your tongue.

I HAVE OATS

for Don Domanski

Stars tendril nearer, droop. Malice.
Two-man-height high tires, industrial, flake down
on a beach south of Campbell River,
three or four bolted together, green-brown bilge sways
in the troughs. The woman renting the cottage near the tires
shivers in dread at them and their powers.
Stone-voiced wind.
A cedar branch slides shrieking
along an eave.

I set it down: I have the farm of 3:00 a.m.;
I have the Zoharic field of weeping, dipping oats.
All true.
But who to say this to?
Snow cutting from the north.
Geese and moon.
Sea lions change sentries.

TREE

The arbutus grows, peeling,
mastodonic, in
the little child's house, he suddenly digests this,
and penetrates the roof over
which its branches spread across torched-on membrane.
He's old enough to assault the lords
they've boxed in a corner of Abraham's dwelling.
The tree terrifies him.
How its red stands out against the white walls of the livingroom.
He gathers saws
and cutlasses, cutlasses and psychological exemptions.
But he quickly notes someone has gone before,
some sleepwalker with a chainsaw, fading, lit hand
and had a go at the greatest branch
so that the tree simply halts, stops
speaking, well above the ground.
What a start to a marriage.

Still, he waters plum trees at the base of the cliff
because they are dry and he wishes
to stop the fire should it roll down the mountain,
its rattling blood scales.

The fruitless plums are his saints, his beds,
which are the jittering, continuous showing of the face
that passes like a river beneath him,
always, quickly under him.

MOON

Full again, warehousing opera,
baled worry, ledges of teeth upended
holding tears, early in morning, headwater
of plugged gravitas, you can barely hear
current crackle as it collects in my neighbour's
maple.
Lightly swollen with crow sulks, wet spider web
one cable touches a cedar
branch, another the lip
of an ice cream bucket
hilled with rain-steeped weeds.

CONTROLLED BURN THEURGY

Scene One, Beginning of the Pandemic

A stream flows out of the head
of the mountain
The stream white waters hummingbirds
A stream out of oaks
Mouth-banked below-the-
tongue slither. Inaugural
river saying, saying
Worded, a stream comes out of the head
of stone cliffs
and from the red moon
bulbing from earth near the volcano
and the volcano's high held snow note
Language of stream
Red moonlight gash on winter Haro Strait
Stream of flowers, camas
Stream of fawn lily, fish flower
Stream of robin, stream of deer
colour of waterlogged wood
Language here plucked
Stream of whales, drift logs

Pray for my Aunt Edna, Uncle Jack and Ronald, the souls' wave, for
Jean, Martin (Louise's cousin) and Louise's
other cousin and her mother
For Peter Butala and Brother Randy, their blowing souls' wave
rivers
Hummingbirds' hammering stream in mountain's thought
Hummingbird in armament and language
The breasts of apple trees
send light paths
The streams in night
The star flows
And language's stalking shimmer
And bees coursing to apple tree breasts

Scene Two

I worried about hummingbirds
in that cold, ice spears
rattling in the feeder I brought
in on the hour
one, male, locked, staring out
of creeping torpor, 4:30 p.m.
in gravid darkening
perched on a stick in a grow box mounted
on the deck railing before
the fluorescent explosion window
A February dream   a doe
noses out a route
behind the kitchen cupboards
and forces her neck and head
through a gap, gouged
hole in one of the doors
I stroke her throat
The new country stands quivering
Its black eye is thrown over me, a tarp

The breasts of apple trees: send light
paths

Charcoal stream in night, cinder-drift
The star flows
send language
as bees make an attempt at apple tree
breasts

Scene Three

Later in prayer
I sit on an orange, 80s, padded, vinyl
rumpus room, gold-legged cocktail stool straddling
a box of unsold copies of *Thinking
and Singing: Poetry and the Practice
of Philosophy*, hay-hooked from drifts
of loose basement matter, one of five boxes
at the tail
end of prayer and look
at the snow-streaked mountain
which assists its rise
to roost in me
How little, how little
I have in my head
The moss, cliff, oaks, wild
plum groaning out of me
All I do
is shuffle my feet

The mountain is dark
The mountain is dark
(fire sent into fire)
Its light is dark
beaming ray of its ceremonies

BOOK I, *REPUBLIC*

Northern Vancouver Island, that throat, elf-dark
past Sayward and the turn off to the Woss sawmill
and the iron mine, equipment abandoned
in forests, someone
in a thin sweater, female,
bends closer to the wood stove, 3:30
a.m. What could justice be?
she wonders. The sea at night, snow
on the highest peaks. She works out
that she will not, at this point,
drink.
A computer holds as lightly as possible
the bombing of Kharkiv, bristling cloth
kept from ruined skin.
Sea lions rustle on the bare rock
island.
A seal bark.

SNOW MOUNTAIN

Right There

The mountain in the robe
of its first skin,
its early, practiced skin, walking
forward skin, enucleated
quiet, a current of sabbath
circling it,
which is a look,
lash-shaded, coming before rock.
The mountain purges
itself of teleologic will
while it builds your eye;
breath of the
blackest bassoon, its hearing
makes an underworld.
The mountain in mystagogic robes
of standing still.

Getting to Snow Mountain

One route to Snow Mountain, the one that opens
both its eyes, is up terraces
behind the balanced-on-a-rock house, along
canals old Mister Hunt put in
in the Sixties to bend iron,
water load shed each winter
by the western face. From there,
it's up the kenotic chimney;
then you trail south along the cliff
base until you find an oak whose trunk has
diverged into five heavy branches, one snapped
by a storm ten winters ago; climb
the southerly branch, touching the
rock wall with your hands and feet
as needed, and you are carried
to the plateau topping the cliff.
The mountain from there is
basaltic verticals, bucks
in rut in the moss.

SNAKE

From the mountain's dark, dropped
belly, grainy gusts beard.
They travel instantly into the elliptical
funnel of your rose.
From snow mountain's careful, careful
weight, filamental dialectic touches
up, spiders up the body inside your body.
The mountain's locked face
plucks a grey stone from your mouth
and places there a red one.
The mountain's hacked quiet-mass
digs into you, shoulders and arms, as it turns
to face the town
in pre-dawn this early December,
red-gold leaves of a winter
plum at the foot
above the submerged, enpiped
river.

It Starts

Pink light smears over the cliff shoulder,
a hummingbird on a blue spruce branch slowly bulbs
from torpor a face pressing and rolled against the under
flesh of *élan vital.*
Snow windrows in fern along the rock.
The great performance, the unbinding, begins.
There is a lifting and a dropping of the tonnage
of what can be seen.
I breathe out clouds into cold air.
There were some knives in the night
carried under clothes by others in the dream.
You could feel their bodies moving
past, humans with herds.

Kenotic Chimney

Down the chimney of kenosis,
slanting headfirst burrow, through light's cave
mud and into the angel's animal mouth,
where your body is spoken,
eaten and spoken,
elongated, studded
with haecceity, its fiery
load.
You grow a gaping plain, it flows
from your shoulders,
are fitted out as a crane migration route
or stone-tipped *quies*
along the mid-island's snow cauled ridge.
Take a seat.

Now this mountain, let's get back to this mountain, your
clever mountain's enfolded body, its glimpse-taste-weight tips
out of its seen body
into your heated core,
it blossoms out for a heated cavity.
You have a stick house in
the desert of the mountain's eye.
You keep a stick house
in the mountain's unoccupied, returning look.

A BLUEBIRD

The uncreated rays of godhead
blew against the boy
to fly under the ground, under the bed of the South
Saskatchewan river curving at Estuary,
abandoned town, sour curtains kicking in three shot out windows.
New sadness   new sadness   he thinks. I do this
for new sadness. The fields burn.
He is stroking, blue,
toward the Alberta border. His sister
Polyhymnia gave him a shove.
The town's sorrow had penetrated drought stiff earth;
he sees it above him now, three yards, hovering
jellyfish, emotional shawl.

New sadness, new sadness,
its caragana shade plating
drags a bomb-curtained room
through his flesh. New sadness,
hand-me-down sadness, grains of tough May snow tick
down in black cliffs,
little sadness, a raccoon rubbing
in his small hands a child's silver cup, new
sadness, an old tooth returning to the jaw.
In a frozen bruised garden a crow
sends word-flash from its tail feathers
Neanderthal? Hittite?
Southern Tutchone?

Into a fissure in rock, Gregory of Nyssa
presses a cloud, no speech beyond this point
the child opens it
with his little tongue
and continues on the rosy
thoroughfare. Wheat fields burn
forests cook air.
He aims to gather
fiery eggs deep in the ground
and by their orange-blue pulse to line up clutter
in his stray European head.

BACK

A muscle of quiet pours
down the mountain's back.
We're in luck.
Angle your mouth for it.
Apophasis's lost tongue.
There. Loop it in, lap it up. Trap it.
Tap it.
Your mouth wing-shaped.
The mountain's rain-rot eye
dark-beaming.
Basalt stylites force out crowns,
flares, uprushing silence.
Travels to the House of Invention,
Norval Morrisseau, falls
down the mountain's back like black hair.
The mountain shimmers, hovers some in magic
stability,
drops its beautiful eyes.

Believe the mountain has flown
to the Ninth Mountain into the hearing
of the Father-King
and from there throws down scented, tangled
emanations back.
Which we climb.
We climb.

BURNING

Wasps corner us where the lawnchairs
nudge the fence and frisk
us for salmon, *hesychia*, aeroplan
points. No one
in the stubby halls of those eyes
walks toward us.
The mandibles dig in flesh
like ours.
One unsticks a dot of gold
ham and stumbles it toward larger air.

65,000 pink and chum come in to spawn
in dried river beds at Bella Bella;
later, invisible
flexions at head height, spirit-thin,
kick back out to sea.
Scream-their-faces-off parties into
the skinny, wee hours around bonfires
bondfires   bone conflagrations
on one of the puckered hills
of Victoria, fireworks'
antlers hissing from its head.

THIS, THEN

The god appears, a breast-
plate of mouths, ears,
eyes, especially eyes, that dinging tongue,
which is also the cliff in its morning fall, sun slicing
the top grass.
Fawns zip
through the yard, fawns
pinball.
Something is up or off; dark
liquid sneaks through cloth; the deer pick it up and swing.
My undertongue heat wave jams
at 39.9 degrees through a week. I fall on the kitchen floor,
responders scrape me off.
A man, in scrubs, his face mask
hanging from an ear
kicks aside the sticky metal lid
to one of the pits
dug under the hospital basement floor
and feeds me in.
Time for a rest, he says.

WRITING ADVANCES FROM THE CLIFF

The doe who died under the cedars
near the road that we carried to the cliff
three weeks ago, gnawed to a grey drift above
oak leaves, has left the lights on in her back hooves and legs
so they stick to our
seeing like drying wax.
The forest predicts multiple days of minus five.
The west side of the mountain in cold, edged rain,
its archival vaults of motionlessness;
in this storehouse lives an owl; you hear
its double-bladed voice scraping as you sit under the reading light
in the shed at 4:30 a.m. Your book is old rain
falling on the whole island and out to sea.

*

On the fire swoon, gold lust last August
in the appetite of hummingbirds, light prickling,
for whatever the old red geranium at the south end
of the car port is selling that pitches, pitches,
cosmos pushes out a nipple.

Hummingbird, deer mouths hive in your chest.

*

We lift her from under cedars
near the road on an ancient shower curtain
up the mountain and roll her off in leaves
beside some Oregon grape
against the lowest cliff. The dead
eyes have us,
nose and jaw
ears and feet.

BITTEN-IN, CLAMPED-ON EAR

The mountain straightens itself again,
as we've come to expect
in its stepping out
hide, a hurled, declared body.
The mountain's exoskeletal breath,
liturgical performance warming up
in blowing snow.

The same wild apple, noumenal fort,
blooms now as it did in Covid March
part way up the rise.
Night soaks away from where people
dumped box springs and one old pay phone
in the new camas.
God's teeth
bite an ear
into poplar bark.

THE *MASSINAHICAN* STREAKS OUT!

Floating masses of text, coagulations,
train cars, thrown, moving at bulking speed,
bending as gusts of crows,
Massinahican, Zohar, The Hidden Eyes of Things,
Roberto Harrison's Tecumseh Republic –
They all streak out!!
Look into the pot they carry inside their quickness,
at simmer, cherry pitch of apokatastasis.
The *Massinahican* streaks out,
Fusus al-hikam streaks out.
Venus in the east. We
meet ourselves in this speed
as north Pacific beaches west of Bear Beach, breakers
knuckling on high shore walls,
fern waving part way up toward us and through us.

UNREPEATABILITY

A moth flies across a November step
Mars aligns in the west.
Vials of *quies* in the guts
of the ballooned rock,
way in, undescriable spearings up, speech, no,
sentences not completely out of matter
above me.
I carry the body of the mountain
a lamb.
The mountain carries my body quickly away
leaving clear, minute rain between the horns
of early hours, the bear of old night roaming.
The mountain's stunning, moral thereness at dawn,
strands of blackberry vine
thrown over igneous spikes
springy with moss.

*

The mountain's onceness, *caritas*
a stake driven into the ground.
Vases of muteness on shelves in the rock produce
fainting.
You are an anthill
of individual fallings down.

The Line of Itinerarium Mentis in Deum

The line, geometrical,
sung solids of Plato, cone, octahedron, tetrahedron,
bobbing in ether bath, cities put out to sea,
is double lane spiration.
The line.
The line triply Forced, cackling
in porcelain conductors.
The line has many homo sapiens's cupboards, doodads and drawers
along its console.
Yet is thinking's flesh escalator. Climb poleward.
The six-winged bird its petroleum asperges.
Goat track through live coals' teeth.
Palace of water
that falls.
Flesh fall.
We ride the mare of logos-Christ
through salal and along beaches.
Flight of Christ-phoenix-carrying-female wake.
The boat on the current of reaching phlogiston.

The House of the Journey of the Mind to God

You endure passage through nettles,
through tied tight air,
through an abandoned shack, decades of shack-life, you endure
    the night journey
and mildly stemmed lightness enters you through spaces
    between wallboards.
Lightness flocking and scattering
its seeds.
Lightness, the turned eye. You begin
a rising   You

Noticing

See how Bonaventura ingresses the created
Great Hall of *Itinerarium Mentis in Deum* where all wear red,
sweeping arms overhead to unshell
a dome, whose name is Francis's ecstatic peace, sparkly
as cetaceous viscera, Francis of Assisi, medicinal blade
of thinking in stilled swoop beside him,
dead thirty-seven years,
the god with his armor of mirrors in super-clear occupation of
  the snowberry.

Out of two or three caves, wet-echoic, animate-black
the line of *Itinerarium Mentis in Deum*,
spiration's old soil,
animals breaching the wall at Niaux,
walking and exhaling out of walls in dear solemnity.

Rushing

What sends the inrush —
"I went into retreat before dawn
and received the illumination before
the sun rose. I remained in this place fourteen months" (Ibn 'Arabi).

Ore cordis, oh my mouth,
climbing hand, one of the Heat's many small mouths
prosthetized in me flies a small plane
toward the sky of glorious showing
discovering a blue rarely seen,
that blue
first mined in the *Phaedrus*,
242 C, the wedding visit of the daimonion, speaking air.

The Roar of Itinerarium Mentis in Deum

The birth of the chest, sweet wound. The breathless emigration,
the line passing into cut grass, harvested oats.
Out of the vase of *Itinerarium Mentis in Deum*
palaces fly
from its brow
deep halls
sweat from
its whirling
in which the feet move free.
Lens placement
of bottomless mind in the occluded eye,
wind, *oculus cordis*, catch and release woo.

EAT

There, the velocity of bird flight
jells in stones in the wall,
stall-quiet in the rock wall.
September light creaks and thunders.
Angelicity *is* a tasting.
The mountain's strict waiting,
meat and sleep, makes little
gestures that stuff streams, currents
of frizzing light food
in us, our flimsy bodies.
The arrow of a look in stones.
The hospital of the Garry oak.
Ingenuity of snowberry
that offers one black hole pill.
Sentience cargoed
milk.
The arbutus who may one day eat up
all anxiety, friend
to mind's damp rind.

CEREMONY

Driving highway 4 south
of Swift Current, ribbed, narrow tar,
aiming for the vacant town of Simmie, west
at the old Metis winter camp at Lac Pelletier,
early evening, and you,
my friend, two hours away, climbing
trees in your new diagnosis;
could be the slough we all end in, road
breaking up until it's no road.
Andy Suknaski country if I go
farther south tonight.
You have to have a fat layer
of a little joy to attempt that place. So
I'll bend west. I spent a morning
trying to find Suknaski's grave in Wood Mountain
a few years back. Lean over the spot, *sir*.
I plan to sleep in the truck in the dead town
of Robsart behind the blown-out, wind-cocked Co-op.
Hello ghosts. Floating,
catching in ditch grass.

OCCULTATION OF KNOWING, LOCALIZATION AND PRESERVATION OF LIGHT

The owl that has softly boomed
through a yard long feathered tube
at 4:10 a.m. in the southeast forest
keeps one story of snow mountain, one
of the bird's few needed tools, and can
say this to next to nobody.
Maybe one night the forest will
take into its cat mouth the single
small person, cousin of a fern?, who is selected
by marriage, slant of light or one cast gaze
to know, who is putting on his stud-buttoned shirt
just now, who is choosing the wide belt
and is ready. No one I know.
I see only the upper skin of the buried sway
of what's going on
not its marrow or theatre
at the drum of the owl
as a gravelly light,
cup of cosmological gruel that would not pour
into any form.
Every breath is a disclosure.

Anger, the sturdy churn
of reason in angels,
circulates above.

WHAT TO DO WITH THE CORAL ROSE?

Alright, ok, Eriugena – I wish he could or would visit
the poor sick coral rose, its pocked, astral faces – wants a sticking,
  unioned
(with God) cosmos (*adunatio*), a Port Mann Bridge breath
joining individuated heat with the beyond-
intelligence torch, touching into sweet sweep
a web, from the secretions of rocks, ants, prints in snow,
  luminescence threaded.
That's alright, fine, I would go for a little breath myself, ripple,
  an absorption,
a little en-housing, a visiting like a sheen growing on cloth,
  the clothing of a form
of life.
  The luciferian gloom of
  acedia's wolfdander, lizard slick – incarcerated in the free self
  anaesthetised by the taste of limitlessness – mouth, mouth
  mouth opening along boredom's back. Nothing nudges.
The *Periphyseon* is in dialogue, launched like a city
of burrowing rodents, spiritual conversation, so, thus, too, an air-
seeking assemblage crowned with rotors that
whip and nip at rising.

When you speak SENĆOŦEN to the young, or even older deer
they stop their flight and turn to look at you and twist and scratch
their backs with their teeth and continue to move from boxwood
to love-lit boxwood. You and they have slipped
behind a doorless wall. Some sort of
Zoharic cone-like room of branches exists in the further back
forest, dark parliament, castle of web
and feather, home-heap of speech and light wind.
The animals see you. You swell from their seeing.
I wish Eriugena would spread the food of just speeches over the
poor coral rose.

VENUS IN THE EAST

Mars, bulbil, in the west, high-hooked
Venus, fleshy, easterly, a
pincer. I'm current-pinned in a lean-to
in the valley between, oaks,
cedars skim my ears, the
naked effulgence of the planets.
Hard frost,
the odor of glaciers still
in earth.

They come,
Bonaventure,
Hypatia, Marguerite Porete,
Damascius, they come again,
come, sit around a pointy
fire on the cliff, some nodding off,
some not speaking, or mouths darkening
as they speak, others speaking
quietly, another chunk of cured blue spruce
clunks onto the burning bed, then
spits a stinging crack.

One of them rolls from a sachet
a death pill, purple green bud,
small hours seed and examines it
in her palm.

HOLY GHOST, AGENT INTELLECT

I go over a fence
I wear teeth on my chest
In my mouth, juices of seditions
I go over a wall
herds flow on the other side
owls with enclawed scrolls float over
Angel, hermeneut of divine silence
Centaurs were here, teaching
with faces of wasps
I carry myself over
Along the soon encountered cliff
mind crackles, then looking up
I see camps and their fires
scatter down a gully   Angel ground
The arbutus speaks across distance
bark of care coming out of warm water
Two tan curls, arbutus peel
skate twenty yards and land
at the high right side of her plate
the day before my wife has surgery on her eye

THE CELESTIAL HIERARCHY

after Pseudo-Dionysius the Areopagite

Above fox moving at night near Valjean, in them
in their tails, above and in coyotes
glare beats, Being-light
voltaic impact, catanyxic, throws
itself down through the triads
rapids, jumping air, beginning with seraphim

they are puffs of mind,
reaching doors o maximal
smoothness
we are in more than a strange city
with them in us   we see it
from what we rake from ash

fire-carriers, outpourings
molten swift the conflagratory
sword (cherubim) whizzing down
and west
Second hierarchy   dominions   *lifting up*
wave of courage   alizarin crimson
Third hierarchy   the drift in luminous

gust
toward the principal

This light that falls in everything
gathers everything   this fox power
returns us back

Domiciles, coveys, cognitive
blinks-of-an-eye, their hush and brush are *potentia*
we smell the intimated
step toward us
as great slippage and fall
the fiery property, the human likeness, the eyes
the nostrils, sense of touch, teeth
electrons, choir, clapping, rivers, joy
angel in the feeling
of being touched on the thigh
is phronesis
We suck on a bogus materiality
and become clear
They are also named as winds, a sign
of the virtually instant speed
pawākan, psychagogic immune system
schola cordis

Above us, below us
raptures of the deep
you swaying to the edge
of the continental roof, hanging
there, see
bug-eyed gardens of nitrogen narcosis
mouths opening in walls
bison-going-over-the-driveline-ledge
euphorias
And with angels – nothingness'
pounds per square inch
peel honeyed mind from us
triggering bloom
bruises, intoxications
the sole body of an
angel

But, O, pink-red hummingbird's darted gorget
and head, air hanging battleship
turning its neck from nowhere and nothing

NO UNTRUE PHILOSOPHY REACHES –

a red room, tongued from a second place, thick
with covenanted mountain ranges,
coastal, reached only by under-rain logging roads, drifting through
dripping, charcoal fir, west shore, Vancouver Island, but
minus stone, so
then a silo of ridgelines of 14,000 foot
quiet.
Nothing true
that does not reach
a metaphysics of ecstasy.

To see or have graze your arm skin
dust of melodic orbital ringing.
Ibn 'Arabi, feet afloat, touches down along the light over-boil African
north rim, leaving utter of an exact noesis, his *peregrinatio*, this whole
  night of it,
all may read.
Or in Castille, rustle of the Companions' talk,
their own feet on roads' stones or inns' stairs
or up to the ankle in garden soil
of 3:30 a.m. where they meet

King David, the donkey driver,
who informs them they are the Lower Reaches
of Eden.

Emerald cities rise and vibrate. Brokenhearted
winds sway their tall buildings until the pollened
tassles of the towers touch one another
and spring back, floured silver with each other's
fertility and interior castle. Our highest in-skinned, below
bone drama-ear
has each their own apartment here, every
resident divine subjectivity and
snowberry in the mouths of deer,
wild carrot a fence of the oak.
Tumbling emanation
cooling, colouring as it passes, whiffs by,
emanational hurtle drunk as a peony,
is only the self. And cut Himalayan
blackberries, the dead oak,
exposed rock.

The ravens squeal to their young,
the percussive small birds. There will be two, one hears,
blasts of the angel's trumpet, one
for the reabsorption of the cosmos

and a four-century sleep, the second
breathes out the long return. Seraphiel
handles the great horn
of flesh and intelligence.
This Eighth climate. The two year
old buck stilling the gold
river torrent of his body
under cedars lies and looks around. Cedar
coop. Wide leaves, floppy maple,
fallen over the dome
of the bush tits' scrotal nest laced to the California lilac
safe from last night's north wind.

Henry Corbin, *Spiritual Body and Celestial Earth: from Mazdean Iran to Shī'ite Iran;* the *Zohar;* Ibn 'Arabi, *Sufis of Andalusia*

FACE

September light in webs and dust
– the Glorifying, the Pure, the Adoring –
Much we have lost, much
emptiness lives through.
The velocity of flight
idles in stones
enstormed in rock.
Snow Mountain appears
out of fog; its body gathers,
a shaken cup of wasps, sheaf
of spiked intelligences.

A rustication in stones busily
at work, a day's travel heavy in stones;
these, wind, fields, bird flight,
assemble a face, un-Cistercian, muddier –

A PAUSE

The child lies
in burn-reachable
mountain grass. Ironwood
in bloom, long air
turkey-tailed
with new storm
curls off the Pacific
burn   wind
frictioning in infinite parts as it somersaults
off sea
catanyxis, X̱IXEX̱E, spiritual
shame tastable
in smoke anticipation.

Mouth inside tastes
torn purple starfish
lapping at the shore
ironwood.

Arrange
yourself, sunken in rock
cleft   staring
straight up at the bottom
of wind
wobbling over.

PORETE

You can see a few lit windows, three or four
in the black towers of the fire
– something is going on in there –
rising over the subdivision.
Within, hysteria grows hands and knits endless liquid red scarves.
We write to you from the nighted interior,
we write to you from the thrall
of this immense personality which is burning
falling on us.

SOCKEYE-MOUTHED FELLOW

turning on it, wheeling
impaled on water's rubbled white back
whorling in fluid metal
it rings, iron, remembering
and sending out worlds from his mouth
the sockeye-mouthed person
thunder of red
compassionate fish flaring below

night eruptions
sea lions flop slovenly
in sleep
on a treeless rock
at the west mouth of active pass
night layered, pounded together, stretching
hummingbirds on winter mountain
dauphinic in ambrosial halls
snow collapses at the height of the malahat
melting as it touches black rock

*

here it is, bitten-in, clamped-on ear

the mountain straightens itself as always now
in its coming forward
skin, rocking wave body
the mountain's girdering breath
warming up
in blurring snow
pushing out a bitten-in ear

the same wild apple, interior room
blooms now like in the first covid month
part way up the rise
evil slant
night soaks away from where people
dumped telephone books and toasters
in new camas
the mountain pushes out a bitten ear

*

when the old british got an idea
to drain maber marsh on the saanich peninsula with steam
shovels and the book of revelation then hang its three streams
    in a meat locker this
ate the common flickers' sense of time and small dogs from whose hair
    blankets were
made took in pains in their legs and
it de-hummed dog salmon tasting the river line at goldstream and dented

whales natally entering at the inlet mouth and detached the retina
of snowberry and fawn lily and deer whose coats are the colour of
  winter ginger fern
and wild cherry and peeling skin of arbutus which, warmed, puts
  its finger
on the tremor in the head and stops it

shenoute, the egyptian, with his still, very
still disciple, returning from the council of ephesus, lost
shot in a shining cloud, flare tipped, overhead and saw
everything that was happening, nothing could be done

*

bisonheaded man, fishtopped man, ҬEKI-mouthed fellow
glued, fitted, to the fighting ear, to achillean hearing, best of
  the centaurs
in a second turning on the sea, lashed
to waves' worming backs at the saanich inlet mouth
at the whale door, blue heron window
in the pre-history of very early morning out on the water, glimpses
language grow from dirt between rocks like grass

PORETE

O, most sweet abyssed one, says Reason,
FineLoved,
falling through the hole
of herself
stoplessly,
tell us the number of deaths, asks Reason,
we must wear
to understand this book.

The Soul is impatient
with all these questions
piled like dirty dishes through the house.
All this work you stack on me,
says the Soul, makes this
book move like a snail.
No one tastes this life, says Porete,
if not dead by all deaths.

"YOU ARE WORTHY TO TAKE THE SCROLL AND TO OPEN ITS SEALS FOR YOU WERE SLAUGHTERED." REVELATION 5:9

The Child says

The deer lay near my head. It
was a night that felt as if another night had come behind it,
then another behind that night, stacking. The deer
rolled on his (her?) shoulder
toward my mouth, this
an ambassadorial gesture, tongue tip of
choosing the long walk
from her place to mine, to spread nerved
speechlessness at my elbow. The deer crackled
through the forest.
I was lying on the ground, then vibrated
up by drums and song tremor.
The deer achieved speed on the highway
of its bright noise. Then it was stretched out almost
touching my arm with its spine through the tarp.
It was night and this was the deer's dreaming. It was music
and the high roof of its freedom.

When another animal, quite famous,
much, much earlier,
with a real history as *the* eloquent animal, with deep
knife marks on it, when that creature
managed to stand without its organs sliding free,
it lifted a fabric revealing
its many, many eyes.
Then it began to weep and read. Read and weep.
Now the deer, this one, comes over to this side
of the river and lies beside me.

NOTES

1. Theurgy is the practice of turning the soul around.
2. *Massinahican* is Louis Riel's lost cosmology.
3. SENĆOŦEN is the language of the W̱SÁNEĆ people and the Saanich Peninsula and the Gulf Islands. (I thank Kevin Paul for teaching me this language, for leading me into its beauty.)
4. SṈAḴE is the true name of Mount Tolmie. In English, this name could be rendered as Snow Mountain.
5. Bonaventure was a follower of St. Francis of Assisi. He wrote a biography of Francis and *Itinerarium Mentis in Deum*, *The Journey of the Mind to God.*
6. The Companions appearing on page 51 are the disciples of Rabbi Shim'on bar Yoḥai in the *Zohar.*
7. Porete is the beguine Marguerite Porete, author of *The Mirror of Simple Souls*. She was executed by fire for the "heresy" of her book.

I thank Sylvia Legris, Jan Zwicky, G.C. Waldrep and Canisia Lubrin for their encouragement.

ACKNOWLEDGEMENTS

pp. 48–50 Pseudo-Dionysius, the Areopagite, *Pseudo-Dionysius, The Complete Works*, translator Colm Luibheid, New York, Paulist Press, 1987, pp. 182 (325D) and 187 (333D).

p. 61 Marguerite Porete, *The Mirror of Simple Souls*, translator Ellen L. Babinsky, New York, Paulist Press, 1993, pp. 130–131.

Author photo: Lia Crowe

TIM LILBURN lives in the Bowker Creek watershed in W̱SÁNEĆ territory on Vancouver Island. He is the author of twelve books of poetry, including *Harmonia Mundi*, *The House of Charlemagne* and *The Names*. His poetry has received the Governor General's Award, the Canadian Authors Association Award, the European Medal of Poetry and Art (the Homer Medal), the Saskatchewan Book of the Year Award and the Cheryl and Henry Kloppenburg Award for Literary Excellence, among other prizes. His poetry has been translated widely. Lilburn is also the author of three earlier essay collections, *Living In The World As If It Were Home*, *Going Home* and *The Larger Conversation: Contemplation and Place*, and editor of two other influential books on poetics. A fourth essay collection, *Numinous Seditions: Interiority and Climate Change*, appeared from the University of Alberta Press in 2023. He has taught at the University of Victoria, the University of Saskatchewan, St. Peter's College and Middlebury College, and worked with the dance company New Dance Horizons/Rouge-gorge as a writer and performer, collaborating with co-directors Edward Poitras and Robin Poitras.